OFFSHORE COMPANIES

OFFSHORE COMPANIES

How to Register Tax-Free Companies in High-Tax Countries

MICHAEL MAGNUSSON

Parts of chapter 4 previously appeared in *The Land without a Banking Law - How to Start a Bank with a Thousand Dollars by Michael Magnusson* (YORK, OPUS OPERIS LLP, 2013). Copyright © 2013 MICHAEL MAGNUSSON. Reprinted with permission.

Published By:

OO
OPUS
OPERIS

OPUS OPERIS LLP
Regency House – Westminster Place
York – YO26 6RW – United Kingdom

Registered in the United Kingdom with Company Number OC381062

We plant a new tree for every printed book we sell.
See www.opusoperis.co.uk for further details.

ISBN: 978-0-9575438-3-6

The government's view of the economy could be summed up in a few short phrases: If it moves, tax it. If it keeps moving, regulate it. And if it stops moving, subsidize it.

Ronald Reagan

CONTENTS

LEGAL NOTICE

If, from the more wretched parts of the old world, we look at those which are in an advanced stage of improvement, we still find the greedy hand of government thrusting itself into every corner and crevice of industry, and grasping the spoil of the multitude. Invention is continually exercised, to furnish new pretenses for revenues and taxation. It watches prosperity as its prey and permits none to escape without tribute.

Thomas Paine

1

Shady versus Sunny

Tax havens have traditionally been politically acceptable as long as they are rainy and cold places such as
Denmark, Delaware, the Netherlands, Ireland and the
United Kingdom. However, if you add a white sand
beach and some palm trees it becomes a different sto-
ry. The tax haven becomes an offensive villain, not
only guilty of "unfair tax competition" but of virtually
every other thinkable evil, including terrorism, money
laundering, and all poverty on planet earth. The fact
that the lion's share of international money laundering
takes place in London and New York, not in the
Caymans or the British Virgin Islands, is usually con-
veniently omitted in any debate on the subject. That

the United States of America is the leading offshore tax haven in the world, with more offshore bank deposits (deposits by non-residents) than Switzerland, is seldom mentioned either.

The United States is the absolute favorite offshore tax haven among Latin American tax evaders and is also popular with Europeans and investors from all over the world for reasons of political stability and strong privacy. Do not think that U.S. authorities automatically share client bank information with the tax authorities in other countries the way they expect those countries to do concerning U.S. clients holding accounts there. The United States offers one of the strongest bank secrecy laws in the world. Financial secrecy in the United States is not more solid than in Switzerland (currently under fierce attack), but it exceeds the level of secrecy offered in Andorra, the Bahamas, Bermuda, the British Virgin Islands, Cyprus, Panama and Turks and Caicos (Source: Tax Justice Network) just to mention a few of the usual suspects in the anti-offshore campaign. The United States is the most popular tax haven in the world for non-Americans, and bank deposits by non-residents exceed US$ 3 trillion.

In times of financial crisis, it is almost irresistible for some politicians to fire cheap rhetorical shots at corporations and the wealthy. When a lot of people (voters) are losing their jobs and homes, political points can easily be scored by adopting the role of a

Robin Hood hero attacking the evil rich. This is nothing new and we see it to a varying degree in every financial crisis. However, in 2013, the extremely low quality of the attacks had me flabbergasted. The shots fired by the United Kingdom and the United States at offshore financial centers this time are so cheap that even the most bitter unemployed couch potato around, for whom they must be intended, should see straight through them. I would respect these politicians if they were actually devoted communists and strongly convinced that private property and enterprise should constitute serious crimes. I would not agree with them, but I would respect their views. They are not Marxists, however, but populist incompetents criticizing matters about which they know nothing in an attempt to score cheap political points.

I felt ashamed to be a member of the human race recently when Apple CEO Tim Cook was bullied and harassed by such politicians in a Senate hearing. Apple is under attack and projected as an evil corporation allegedly not paying its "fair share." In this particular case, the rainy tax haven of Ireland plays a major role in the controversy, rather than any white sand beach counterpart. So what has Apple done wrong? Did they cook the books Enron style? Absolutely not, and not even the most ignorant politicians are suggesting that they did. And yet, Apple is accused of being offshore tax dodgers. I think we can all agree that Apple is a truly global operation and that they are not merely pretending to be one to access cross border tax avoidance opportunities. As we all know Apple manufactures iPhones, iPads and other global best sellers in China. Apple maintains an Irish subsidiary in which part of the profits from global (non-U.S.) sales are accumulated. This subsidiary pays little tax in Ireland. So is Ireland upset about this? Certainly not. Ireland has created an offshore financial center specifically to attract international corporations, among which Apple must be considered as bona fide as they come. Nonetheless, politicians in the United States are upset and accuse Apple of not paying taxes, of being offshore tax dodgers not paying their "fair share" at home. Note that we are talking about overseas sales here, not U.S. sales of Apple products. Apple has accumulated large amounts of cash in their Irish subsidiary from non-U.S. sales, and the U.S. politicians in question now have the audacity to call it immoral that Apple does not immediately bring all those profits "home" and pay 35 percent federal corporate income tax on the same. I should mention that most of the cash owned by the Irish Apple subsidiary is in fact being invested in U.S. securities and assets already and hence fueling the U.S. economy.

Think about how easy it would be for a corporation like Apple to pay almost no U.S. tax at all. They could export their products (which are produced mainly in China) to the United States from offshore subsidiaries using pricing that could limit or even eliminate the taxable profits from U.S. operations. They could keep their designers and product developers in California but accumulate profits, including those generated in the United States, in any tax haven of their choice (subject to transfer pricing regulations, of course). They are not doing this. They have in fact become the largest corporate income tax payer in America, paying US$ 6 billion to the US Treasury in 2012. This fact is ignored entirely in all political attacks on Apple that I have witnessed so far. Apple was founded in a garage in 1976 and has grown to be the most valuable company in the world. It employs eighty thousand people directly and many more indirectly. If Apple can be accused of being a burden on society and an evil corporate beacon of greed by audacious politicians living off tax-payer-funded incomes, then who is safe from such attacks?

Apple is simply using international corporate structuring to avoid paying more tax than necessary on their global profits. It would be negligent and nothing short of financial malpractice for a corporation not to consider taxes a cost as any other. It is the responsibility of any corporation toward its shareholders to avoid paying more taxes than legally required. Many more companies are under attack, and not only in the United States. But I think Apple serves as one of the better examples of how political and absurd the "War on Tax Havens" has become.

The global offensive against the use of tax havens was recently boosted by the controversial leak of more than 2 million stolen records, revealing private information about bank deposits, corporate structures, trusts, and other confidential information. The information comes mainly from warm and sunny tax havens, not from any cold and rainy ones. The Washington-based International Consortium of Investigative Journalists (ICIJ) proudly published a substantial part of this leaked information in a public online database, including private home addresses of corporate officers and other principals in more than 170 countries. Do not get me wrong; I am against tax evasion (but not legal tax avoidance), just as I am against money laundering, fraud, and other crimes, and of course, authorities should fight crime. Nonetheless, I think it is very worrying when the theft of confidential information is not only considered morally acceptable but even praised as the most efficient and preferred method of gathering confidential data, on criminals and innocents alike. Privacy and secrecy laws exist in nearly every civilized country for good and legitimate reasons.

The ICIJ database website starts with the following disclaimer:

There are legitimate uses for offshore companies and trusts. We do not intend to suggest or imply that any persons, companies or other entities included in the ICIJ Offshore Leaks Database have broken the law or otherwise acted improperly.

And yet they put them (or us, rather, because I am also included) all out there in the database "hall of shame," complete with home addresses and details about highly private structures, including family trusts and foundations, all gathered from stolen documents. Offshore critics argue that such information should be public in the first place. It should be noted that in the United States, where the ICIJ is based, such information can be kept 100% private and does not form part of any public record.

The fact is that typical warm and sunny tax havens are required by law since many years back to clearly identify the beneficial owners and principals of all legal entities established there. The disclosure requirements and anti-money laundering provisions far exceed those of the United Kingdom and the United States. Anyone looking for financial privacy and strong secrecy, criminal or not, is much better off in Delaware than in the British Virgin Islands. Nevertheless, much of the information posted in the public ICIJ database, including from the British Virgin Islands, should simply not be public, and again, in the United States, where the ICIJ is based, it never would be.

I see nothing shady about preferring to keep one's financial affairs private. Why is it that information about our financial assets should be in the public domain in the name of transparency? If it is morally acceptable to steal and publish someone's bank statements and legal documents, is it also acceptable to steal and publish someone's love letters or medical records? Why do we not have the right to keep our private affairs, well, private?

I found it absurd already as a child growing up in Sweden that people could and would buy a thick publication called the "taxation calendar" (Taxeringskalendern). The publication looks like a phone book, but instead of using it to look up someone's phone number, you use it to look up the person's income. The website promoting the latest edition encourages you to "check your colleagues, neighbors and friends." The publication even includes a list with the top earners in each county, complete with home addresses for burglars, kidnappers, and others to use as they see fit. The absurd extent to which transparency was always touted in Sweden certainly played a role in triggering my early interest in the world of offshore finance.

There are obviously legitimate reasons for privacy and for not keeping all of your assets in one jurisdiction, however stable the economy and political situation might appear in your home country at any given time. In most countries, assets can be seized at the push of a button because of a tax audit, a frivolous law suit, or a false accusation of a crime. In what can be considered less civilized countries, assets can be seized based on race, political beliefs, or sexual orientation. The seizure of assets could severely impede your capability to fight back, when you need your assets the most.

If it were not for Swiss bank secrecy, the Nazis would have succeeded in seizing virtually all assets owned by Jews in Europe in the 1930s. Financial privacy and secrecy can play a crucial role in protecting our most basic civil liberties and human rights. It would be extremely naïve to think that the world in which we now live has changed in such ways that privacy is no longer legitimately required.

Bank secrecy can obviously be lifted when someone is under investigation for a crime. However, the situation we see more and more frequently is not the lifting of secrecy provisions in criminal investigations but rather scenarios in which the authorities "harvest" massive amounts of data about people who are not under any type of investigation. The data have typically been acquired on what is becoming an increasingly lucrative market, namely, the market for stolen confidential banking information. The thieves, who prefer to call themselves "whistle blowers," are often bank employees supposedly concerned about possible tax evasion among their clientele. They steal confidential data from their employers, extract client lists sorted according to nationality, and then contact the tax authorities in each respective country and attempt to squeeze out the highest possible bid for the loot, all in the name of transparency and justice, of course.

In my opinion, tax evasion should be combated just as other crimes. The authorities should abide by the laws that it is their duty to uphold and enforce. Thieves should be prosecuted, not celebrated as heroes. While stealing is rewarded with tens of millions in "whistle blower" fees (tax-payer funded), tax cheats go to prison.

At the time I write this both Dolce and Gabbana have just been sentenced to twenty months in prison for tax evasion, and Grammy-winning singer Lauryn Hill just started to serve her three month sentence in a federal prison in Connecticut for failure to report a part of her income (which she later reported and paid taxes on in full). Could heavy fines not suffice to punish such crimes? Financial incentive is, after all, the motivator for tax evasion in the first place. A severe monetary punishment should therefore be rather effective in deterring further evasion. Or do we need to keep tax evaders off the streets for reasons of public safety?

The conclusions one can draw from the current political climate, the bullying of small, sunny tax haven countries and the political propaganda with regard to offshore finance are several. First of all, it is more important than ever to have your house in order when it comes to asset protection and tax avoidance structures. You might not have any intentions to share the details of your legal and financial structuring with the public, but you should certainly be prepared for the possibility of having to do so.

Simply to hide untaxed money in a foreign bank account and hope that bank secrecy takes care of the rest is obviously not and never was a legitimate tax avoidance strategy.

You might also want to take a good look at cold and rainy tax havens. You can certainly come under attack even if you avoid white sand beaches in your jurisdictional selection and even if you follow every possible law and regulation in your home country and everywhere else (look at Apple). It is, however, much less fashionable to attack the gray and rainy tax havens, and for this reason, I think they are more attractive than ever. Why structure a simple tax-free company for international trading activities or holding purposes on a small tropical rock in the ocean if you know for a fact that such rocks so intensely upset journalists, tax inspectors, and left-field propagandists, among others? If everyone from your accountant and his grandmother to the prime minister of the United Kingdom of Great Britain and Northern Ireland are relentlessly critical about corporate structuring under the palm trees, this is a valid reason to consider incorporating elsewhere.

If you are looking for financial privacy and tax freedom, you can find this in the cold countries that like to call the warmer tax havens "sunny places for shady people." The most notorious tax haven criticism comes from the most prominent offshore tax havens in the world, the United States and the United Kingdom. I focus on the quite attractive tax-free corporate structures for offshore activities available in those two countries in this book. And for good measure I throw in New Zealand. Although New Zealand cannot be considered one of the big bullies in the political attacks on offshore financial centers and tax havens, the nation categorically denies being a tax haven itself. Tax haven or not, one thing is for certain: offshore income in a New Zealand company owned by non-residents can certainly enjoy a zero rate of taxation.

New Zealand also offers tax-free secretive offshore trusts. General capital gains tax, inheritance tax and estate taxes are nonexistent, and it is not even gray and rainy all the time.

I hope you enjoy reading this book. I always welcome feedback and any questions you might have.

Michael Magnusson
readers@michaelmagnusson.com

Philosophy teaches a man that he can't take it with him;
taxes teach him he can't leave it behind either.

Mignon McLaughlin
The Second Neurotic's Notebook

2

United States of America

The United States is a sharp and frequent critic of sunny offshore tax havens. What is often omitted in the propaganda is the fact that the most prominent corporate tax haven of them all is located fewer than one hundred miles from the White House, and it is not a rock in the ocean framed by white sand beaches. Delaware is home to more corporations than people, 945,326 versus 897,934 on the last count. The state offers one of the most business-friendly environments in the world. More infamous jurisdictions, such as the Republic of Panama, copied and adopted the corporate legislation of Delaware straight off.

You can incorporate a new company in Delaware in less than one hour, and the registry stays open until midnight on Monday to Thursday and until half past ten at night on Fridays. Have you ever seen such eagerness to attract new business in the Caribbean?

More than 50 percent of all public corporations in the United States are incorporated in Delaware, including more than 60 percent of the Forbes 500 companies. Delaware does not impose any state corporate income tax if a corporation does not have any local operations or income. Most corporations incorporated in Delaware have no physical presence at all in the state. Just as in the case of other U.S. states, little to no effort is made to identify the owners and principals of a corporation. This would be unthinkable in, for example, Caribbean tax havens, where disclosure and anti-money laundering measures are much stricter, in part as a result of international political pressure (including from the United States).

What many incorporators and offshore service providers forget to tell their international clients is that although the corporation may not be required to pay state income tax or to file a state tax return, all U.S. corporations are required to file a *federal* tax return and to pay 35 percent federal income tax on their worldwide income (tax discounts apply for taxes paid overseas), regardless of in which state they were incorporated.

I have frequently met Europeans operating regular Delaware corporations thinking that they are not required to file any tax returns or to pay any taxes on non-U.S. source income. Such non-compliance can have very serious consequences.

The tax-free solution for international operations is the limited liability company (LLC). An LLC is not a partnership or a corporation but a unique legal entity form of its own. It combines the corporate advantage of limited liability with the partnership advantage of tax transparency. This means that the LLC itself is not assessed for tax. The members (owners) are responsible for any applicable taxation on their part of the profits, as in a partnership. A U.S. LLC with no U.S. operations, no U.S.-source income, and only non-resident members is not subject to federal income tax and is not required to file a U.S. tax return. An LLC owned from offshore and with no U.S. income can consequently enjoy complete tax freedom. LLC members (minimum of one) can very well be offshore entities from zero-tax jurisdictions.

Although the LLC is not required to file a U.S. tax return if it has no U.S. income or operations, it is still required, just as any other U.S. person, to file a Report of Foreign Bank and Financial Accounts (FBAR) with the IRS if it holds any account outside the United States with a balance of more than US$ 10,000 at any given time. Accounts subject to FBAR reporting include bank accounts, brokerage accounts, mutual fund holdings, trust accounts, and any other type of non-U.S. financial accounts. The FBAR reporting requirement is seldom mentioned by incorporators and offshore service providers marketing Delaware structures to international clients, even though it is absolutely crucial to comply with this requirement. It would clearly defy the purpose of establishing a U.S. tax-free structure for offshore operations just to violate IRS reporting requirements and become subject to heavy fines or worse. Failing to file FBARs can be a criminal offence subject to fines of up to US$500,000 and prison terms of up to ten years. In civil FBAR cases, each non willful FBAR violation draws a US$10,000 fine and each willful violation the greater of US$100,000 or 50 percent of the amount in the account. Each year you fail to file counts as a separate violation.

It might seem illogical to require an entity that is not subject to U.S. taxation to report details about all its non-U.S. bank accounts to the IRS. Nonetheless, this is mandatory.

The relevant form (TD F 90-22.1) and instructions for FBAR reporting can be accessed here:

www.irs.gov/pub/irs-pdf/f90221.pdf

The first step in forming an LLC is to choose a company name and verify that the name is not deceptively similar to that of any existing Delaware business entity. A name availability search can be performed on this webpage:

delecorp.delaware.gov/tin/EntitySearch.jsp

Under Delaware law the LLC name must contain the words Limited Liability Company or the abbreviation LLC.

The LLC is created by filing a Certificate of Formation (see sample on the following page) with the Delaware Division of Corporations and payment of the US$90 filing fee.

UNITED STATES OF AMERICA

STATE of DELAWARE
LIMITED LIABILITY COMPANY
CERTIFICATE of FORMATION

First: The name of the limited liability company is

Second: The address of its registered office in the State of Delaware is   in the City of
     Zip code   . The name of its Registered Agent at such address is

Third: (Use this paragraph only if the company is to have a specific effective date of dissolution: "The latest date on which the limited liability company is to dissolve is.")

Fourth: (Insert any other matters the members determine to include herein.)

In Witness Whereof, the undersigned have executed this Certificate of Formation this

     day of

                    By:

                    Authorized Person(s)

                    Name:

The LLC must appoint an agent for service of legal process in the state, referred to as the registered agent. The registered agent can be either an individual or a business entity. The address used must be a physical street address located in the state of Delaware.

You can find a list of registered agents on the following web page:

corp.delaware.gov/agents/agts.shtml

Note that registered agents in Delaware are not regulated by the state or subject to qualification and licensing requirements as they are in other typical offshore jurisdictions. The only legal requirements a Delaware registered agent needs to satisfy is to be located in the state and be open during normal business hours for the purpose of accepting legal service of process.

A Delaware LLC is not required to have an operating agreement but it is highly recommended to create one. There is no requirement to file the operating agreement (in case you create one) with the Certificate of Formation. If you do not have an operating agreement your LLC will be governed by the default rules as stipulated by state law. Your operating agreement can overrule such default rules and instead dictate rules that apply to your specific circumstances. In an LLC with more than one member, this can be crucial to avoid misunderstandings and conflicts further down the road with regard to profit and loss sharing, voting powers, new member appointments, and member departures, just to mention a few examples.

Most banks, especially outside the United States will require more company documentation than just a certificate of formation when you apply for a new account, and the operating agreement will usually satisfy such requirements. The document serves the same purpose as the articles of incorporation in a regular corporation.

Most LLC operating agreements include provisions with regard to the following:

- Percentage interests of the members

- Rights and obligations of the members

- Member voting powers

- Management of the LLC

- Profit and loss allocations

- Rules for member meetings and votes

- Buyout provisions regulating the procedure to follow when a member wants to sell his or her interest or a member dies.

A sample LLC operating agreement is located at the end of this book.

An LLC with more than one member is required to apply for an employer identification number (EIN) from the IRS, even if it does not have any employees.

The EIN is very easy and completely free to obtain directly from the IRS. Beware of providers trying to charge high fees for EIN applications. If you plan to open U.S. bank accounts for your LLC, you will need the EIN, because no bank will open an account without one.

The easiest way to apply for the EIN is online. However, the online option is only possible if the authorized person filing the application has a tax payer identification number such as an EIN, Social Security number or individual taxpayer identification number (ITIN) already. If you are a non-U.S. person with no U.S. tax identification number, you can apply by phone, fax, or mail by filling out form SS-4. I strongly recommend that you prepare by filling out the form even if you apply by phone because this will make the conversation with the IRS agent more streamlined. The EIN is assigned and given to you over the phone.

If you apply by fax, the EIN will be faxed back to you within four days. If you apply by mail, it will be delivered by mail within four weeks.

Form SS-4 and full instructions can be accessed here:

www.irs.gov/Businesses/Small-Businesses-&-Self-Employed/How-to-Apply-for-an-EIN

Rather than filing your own Certificate of Formation with the secretary of state you will probably prefer to engage the services of a company formation agent that also serves as a Delaware registered agent. As previously mentioned, do not expect the formation agent to provide much advice with regard to your obligations or on the subject of international taxation. Most providers like to boast about all the benefits of Delaware as a corporate haven, and they actively try to attract non-U.S. customers. But the after-sales support can be very limited, so be sure to check whether the agent can provide the services you require before you proceed. Some agents offer complete virtual office services, whereas others only provide the registered office address for official communications.

Others offer add-on services, such as accounting and opening of bank accounts and merchant accounts.

I include contact details for a few providers of incorporation and registered office services here for your convenience, but you can easily find many hundreds more online. The fees are generally very low when compared to more typical offshore jurisdictions, with some agents charging a mere US$10 to handle your incorporation. As in most business sectors in the United States, competition is fierce, and no company formation agent in Delaware expects to make thousands or even hundreds of dollars on a single incorporation.

The Corporate Plaza
800 Delaware Avenue
P.O. Box 8702
Wilmington, DE 19899
Phone: 1-302-652-7580
Toll-free: 1-888-279-9100
Fax: 1-302-652-8597
info@delawarecorp.com
www.delawarecorp.com

Agents and Corporations, Inc.
1201 Orange Street, Suite 600
Wilmington, DE 19801

Phone: 1-302-575-0877
Toll-free: 1-800-759-2248
Fax: 1-302-575-1642
agents@incnow.com
www.incnow.com

Harvard Business Services, Inc.
16192 Coastal Highway
Lewes, DE 19958
Phone: 1-302-645-7400
Toll-free: 1-800-345-CORP
Fax: 1-302-645-1280
info@delawareinc.com
www.delawareinc.com

Although I focus on Delaware here, the tax-transparent LLC is not in any way restricted to this state. The same tax benefits for offshore activities can be found in several other states. Delaware is the best known U.S. corporate tax haven, but this fact in itself might be a reason why you would like to consider another state for your LLC. The procedures and costs are very similar throughout the United States and the LLC operating agreement sample included in this book is not state specific.

In the following, I list the most popular states for off-shore purposes and the annual franchise tax/license fee that an LLC must pay to remain in legal good standing:

Delaware	US$250
Wyoming	US$50
Oregon	US$100
New Jersey	US$50
New York	No fee
Florida	US$140
Washington, D.C.	US$165 (every 2 years)
Arkansas	US$150

I personally find New York a quite attractive LLC jurisdiction. There is no annual franchise tax to pay, and few locations can compete with New York City when it comes to global recognition and prestige. If you are image conscious, you can very well set up an LLC with a registered address on Wall Street or Fifth Avenue by spending a few hundred dollars on a mail-forwarding service. Major international banks are obviously present in New York, and it is, in my opinion, a very pleasant place to visit for business and pleasure alike. I include contact details for a few providers that offer services in various states here, but just as in the case of Delaware, you can find hundreds more online:

MyCorporation Business Services, Inc
23586 Calabasas Rd., Suite 102
Calabasas, CA 91302
Phone: 1-818-224-7639
Toll-free: 1-877-MY-CORP-2
Fax: 1-818-879-8005
www.mycorporation.com

Companies Incorporated
28015 Smyth Drive
Santa Clarita, CA 91355
Phone: 1-661-253-3303
Toll-free: 1-800-830-1055
Fax: 1-661-259-7727
www.companiesinc.com

BizFilings
8040 Excelsior Dr., Suite 200
Madison, WI 53717
Phone: 1-608-827-5300
Toll-free: 1-866-265-6133
www.bizfilings.com

UNITED STATES OF AMERICA

USA Corporate Services Inc.
19 W. 34th Street, Suite 1021
New York, NY 10001
Phone: 1-212-239-5050
Fax: 1-212-239-5319
www.usa-corporate.com

Blumberg Excelsior
16 Court Street, 14th Fl.
Brooklyn, NY 11241
Phone: 1-212-431-5000
Fax: 1-800-561-9018
weborders@blumb.com
www.blumberg.com

I don't know if I can live on my income or not;
the government won't let me try it.

Bob Thaves

3

United Kingdom

The United Kingdom has perhaps become the sharpest critic of them all in the global campaign against tax havens. At the time of writing, Prime Minister David Cameron seems to have decided that the best way for the United Kingdom to avoid becoming a prime target in the offensive (many offshore tax havens are after all British overseas territories), is to spearhead the campaign and shout the loudest about the evils of illegal tax evasion and legal tax avoidance alike. This strategy has consisted mainly of cheap rhetoric political attacks. Cameron has also written letters to his overseas territories asking them to commit to some vague agenda of increased transparency. Although

Cameron has boasted about his letter-writing activities at G-8 meetings, no one seems to be clear on what exactly should be changed, if anything at all. Offshore tax havens have required identification of beneficial owners and principals for many years, long before the United Kingdom finally implemented such requirements "onshore" by passing their Money Laundering Regulations in 2007.

The whole campaign gets rather embarrassing every time the British press reveals offshore tax avoidance strategies deployed by Cameron's colleagues, political allies, and opposition alike. Every politician seems eager to join the populist anti-offshore campaign without considering that his or her own Isle of Man trusts and Gibraltar property holding companies might make him or her look rather hypocritical.

Perhaps the most concrete action Cameron wants to take is to impose a new public registry revealing the final beneficial ownership of every U.K. Company.

I just wonder if the transparency fanatics really can comprehend what this venture would entail. First of all, let me clarify that beneficial ownership information with regard to private companies is not publicly available anywhere in the world, not in one single country. The media often makes it sound as if typical rock-in-the-ocean tax haven nations are somehow the ones offering this "veil of secrecy" by not publicly disclosing beneficial ownership details, thereby promoting abuse involving evil shell corporations. But the reality is that no country in the world maintains a public registry with beneficial ownership information. Not even in transparency-obsessed Sweden have they gone that far. Lawmakers in the United States have proposed several bills to require that beneficial owners of companies be made public, but these proposals have made no progress whatsoever in the U.S. Congress.

Even if many countries have banned the use of anonymous "bearer shares," they do not publicly disclose beneficial ownership. Ironically, the United Kingdom is one of the few jurisdictions still allowing for anonymous bearer shares. A U.K. ban on bearer shares would be logical and will surely be implemented sooner or later. However, the implications of creating and maintaining a public registry with beneficial ownership details would no doubt serve to make the United Kingdom one of the most bureaucratic and least business-friendly countries in the world. I do not think even Cameron will allow for that to happen, and my bet is that the UK will remain a relatively business friendly jurisdiction for the foreseeable future. Time will prove me right or wrong.

Let us move on from the political circus and hypocritical campaigns and instead take a look at what the United Kingdom actually has to offer for offshore operations.

Just as in the United States, the most attractive entity for offshore operations in the United Kingdom is also a tax-transparent entity, namely, the limited liability partnership, LLP. The LLP is a hybrid between a limited company and an ordinary partnership, offering the members limited liability whilst retaining the flexibility and tax transparency of a partnership.

A U.K. LLP is formed by two or more members who can be physical individuals or legal entities of any nationality and resident anywhere in the world. The members will have no U.K. tax liability if they are non-U.K. residents and the income in the LLP is not derived from a U.K. source. The LLP then files a "NIL" tax return. Members obviously need to comply with their tax obligations in their countries of tax residence.

Members can very well be offshore companies from more traditional tax havens. The LLP is not required to have a member's agreement, but it is highly recommended to create one, just as in the case of the U.S. LLC.

A LLP member's agreement would typically include the following:

- The name of the LLP

- Whether the registered office is to be situated in England or Wales or both.

- The activities of the LLP

- The method for appointing new members

- The system for removing problem members

- The system for dealing with deceased members

- How the capital cost is reimbursed when a member dies or leaves the LLP

- When and how profits are divided

- How much is contributed to the debts of the LLP on winding up

- Names of members on incorporation

- Minimum and maximum number of members

- Date of commencement of the agreement

- Outline of the duties of members

- Restrictions on members in respect of competition and confidentiality

- Detailed provisions for outgoing members and possible non-competition provisions.

- Insurance and pensions

- Notice provisions to members

- Procedure at meetings

- Votes of members

You can find LLP agreement templates online or let a U.K. lawyer draft one for you. An example of a standard template can be found on this site:

www.compactlaw.co.uk/limited-liability-partnership-agreement.html

The LLP can engage in any lawful commercial activity. It must operate for profit and can thus not be used for charitable purposes.

Financial accounts and an annual return must be filed with the company register, the Companies House. If the LLP profit exceeds GBP 200,000, the amount attributable to the member with the largest profit share must be disclosed.

An audit is only required if more than two of the following limits are exceeded:

- More than fifty employees

- Turnover greater than GBP 6.5 million

- Gross assets of more than GBP 3.26 million

Some of my clients who were looking to establish a U.K. presence without missing out on the tax benefits of the LLP, chose to establish a regular UK limited company and have this company act as a minority member in the LLP with a 5 percent share. The remaining 95 percent ownership interest would be held by a tax-free offshore company from a traditional tax haven such as the Seychelles. In this scenario the U.K. limited company act as an administration company or managing partner. This provides for a solid U.K. presence and yet 95 percent of the profits in the LLP would not be subject to U.K. taxation. The minority member would pay 20 percent U.K. corporate tax on its 5 percent share of the LLP profits, of course after deducting the costs for running the U.K. administration office.

In my opinion the U.K. LLP is one of the most attractive structures available for operations with non-U.K. source income.

To form a Company in the United Kingdom costs very little compared to the costs in typical offshore jurisdictions. Just as in the United States the competition is fierce, and you can find hundreds of providers online charging virtually nothing to form your company. However, make sure to check what the ongoing fees will be, because many incorporators make up for low setup fees with exorbitant ongoing maintenance fees. You will need a registered office in England or Wales and usually this is provided by the incorporation firm for an annual fee. You might want the same firm to provide accounting services and to file the annual return and accounts with the Companies House.

The registration fee for a U.K. LLP is GBP 40 if you file for LLP incorporation yourself using the paper form LL IN01 available here:

www.companieshouse.gov.uk/forms/formsContinuat ion.shtml#LLIN01

There is a same-day service option available for GBP 100. Most incorporators use special software for Companies House filings and the fees applicable for electronic incorporation are significantly lower, at GBP 13 for a standard LLP filing and GBP 30 for same-day service. Sometimes you can therefore see incorporators offering LLP formations for less than what you would pay when filing directly with the Companies House yourself using paper forms.

A complete LLP guide and FAQ can be found here:

companieshouse.gov.uk/about/gbhtml/gpllp1.shtml

Following are the contact details of a few incorporators offering LLP registration and associated services:

Legal Clarity Ltd.
Cornwall Buildings
45-51 Newhall Street
Birmingham
B3 3QR
Phone: +44 121 222 4230
customerservice@legalclarity.co.uk
www.legalclarity.co.uk

Apex Company Services Ltd.
46 Syon Lane
Osterley
TW7 5NQ
Phone: +44 20 8568 6785
Fax: +44 20 8569 8886
info@eformations.co.uk
www.eformations.co.uk

ABS All Business Solutions Ltd.
Office 11
10 Great Russell Street
London
WC1B 3BQ
Phone: +44 207 193 6059
Fax: +44 207 193 6059
info@companyinuk.co.uk
www.companyinuk.co.uk

Complete Formations
Third Floor
207 Regent Street
London
W1B 3HH
Phone: +44 207 1181 800
Fax: +44 207 7882 934
info@completeformations.co.uk
www.completeformatins.co.uk

@UK Plc
5 Jupiter House
Calleva Park
Aldermaston
Reading
Berkshire
RG7 8NN
Phone: +44 118 963 7000
Fax: +44 118 963 7012
www.ukplc.com

You must pay taxes. But there's no law
that says you gotta leave a tip.

Morgan Stanley advertisement

4

New Zealand

The authorities in New Zealand sometimes behave in mysterious ways. They often seem paranoid or terrified of anything "offshore," while at the same time they appear to be incredibly naïve when it comes to international compliance. Practically all jurisdictions worldwide, and certainly most typical offshore tax havens, have implemented extensive requirements for identifying beneficial owners and principals of companies and other legal structures for many years. If you have formed a company or opened a bank account "offshore" during the last decade or two you will be familiar with these requirements. Companies in most jurisdictions are required to have a locally licensed resident agent for record keeping and for the provision of a registered office and address for legal service. The agent is normally required to identify all principals of a company prior to formation and to verify their residential addresses. Some jurisdictions go further by requiring professional references and letters of introduction from any new clients. Any tax haven jurisdiction that does not comply with what have become internationally accepted procedures for client identification and prevention of money laundering would find itself on numerous international blacklists. So what about New Zealand? Somehow New Zealand missed all these worldwide compliance developments worldwide and has continued their business as if they had never heard about "Know Your Customer" and anti-money laundering (AML) measures implemented in nearly every other nation on earth. I should mention that the United States and the United Kingdom can also be considered among the more lax countries in this department.

New Zealand did not implement the Anti-Money Laundering and Countering Financing of Terrorism Act that they finally passed in 2009 until mid-2013. Imagine a small tax haven country not having an AML act in force in early 2013. The tax haven in question would find itself on every possible blacklist around the world and be completely slaughtered by the media. There would be accusations of intentional sponsoring of international drug running and terrorism and pretty much every other imaginable evil of the world. Some reporters and bloggers are so incredibly angry at tax havens that they would not miss such an opportunity. I often wonder if it really is "unfair tax competition" that fuels all this anger towards offshore tax havens. One thing is for certain: a country like New Zealand, which is not generally considered an evil tax haven by the anti-offshore crowd, even though it offers plenty of tax-free structures for offshore activities, can get away with extreme blunders when it comes to international compliance and AML. One of these extreme blunders was New Zealand's idea of setting up an online incorporation interface through which anyone, anywhere in the world, could incorporate a New Zealand company almost instantly at a total cost of about NZ$150, and with no requirement to identify directors, shareholders, or any other party in the process. Any offshore tax haven country even considering setting up such a service would most likely end up with more international sanctions than Iran.

New Zealand eventually woke up and smelled the coffee, but only after a lot of noise had been made. In 2009, a New Zealand company was incorporated online for the purpose of chartering a Georgian (the former Soviet Republic state, not the U.S. state) registered cargo plane and using it to smuggle thirty-five tons of illegal weapons from North Korea to Thailand. Later, a Justice Ministry Report in New Zealand estimated that New Zealand shell companies were used to launder NZ$ 1.5 billion every year. This was all because of the ease with which one could register a New Zealand company online without any identification procedures.

Links were found between New Zealand shell companies and the Russian Mafia and Mexico's Sinaloa drug cartel as well as North Korean arms trading. Each time a new scandal blew up in the New Zealand press, the government would send out what seemed to be the same old press release, time after time, announcing that new tough rules would be adopted to stop the abuse.

So what exactly would these tough rules entail?

The proposed changes initially included some sort of resident agent requirement for each company. The government seemed to seriously discuss this issue as if they were about to invent the wheel and appeared blissfully unaware of the fact that the concept was invented a very long time ago. The final outcome seems to be that all New Zealand companies will be required to have at least one resident director or a director resident in a trusted, non-scary country abroad. So far, the only non-scary country to which they are considering granting this trusted status is, yes, you guessed it, their big brother Australia.

Smaller tax haven countries must be observing New Zealand and wondering how on earth a country can get away with all these self-inflicted disasters. As I have already pointed out, any tax haven behaving like this would no doubt be severely punished. New Zealand has so far gotten away with the European Union taking it off the banking and corporate "white list" in mid-2012. Some people in New Zealand perceived this as a major blow. If they only knew how lightly they had gotten away.

While law-makers are lagging behind, the Companies Office has proactively decided to start requesting certified copies of government-issued identification and utility bills (as proof of residential address) from directors and shareholders of new companies. Although they forget to ask for identification in some cases, this will become a standard requirement, at least in cases of non-resident directors and shareholders.

Note that you can still file for incorporation online. The process has changed only in that the Companies Office will hold your application for incorporation until you have provided copies of identification and proof of address.

Another embarrassing blunder by the New Zealand Companies Office was its decision in 2010 to implement new company name restrictions. These restrictions were enforced without any change of legislation, regulation, or anything else to support such action.

Many companies had been incorporated using the word "Bancorp" or "Bancorporation" in the company name. These names had obviously been duly approved by the Companies Office prior to incorporation. All jurisdictions have clear regulations concerning restricted words that cannot be used in company names. Although amendments can obviously be made to such regulations, I have never seen a company registration authority suddenly invent new restrictions of its own accord, forcing existing companies to change their names without any legislative grounds for forcing them to do so.

Typically, new regulations regarding name restrictions apply only to new incorporations and not to existing companies, for what ought to be obvious reasons. However, New Zealand chose to be different than the rest of the world in this regard as well. The Companies Office arbitrarily decided that "Bancorp" and "Bancorporation" were derivatives of the restricted word "Bank" because such words include the letters "banc", which, according to the Companies Office, translates as "bank" in a foreign language. It did not specify in which language "banc" was supposed to be the word for "bank," nor did it explain why it had approved the allegedly restricted company names in the first place. For example, in the United States, the words "banc" and "bancorp" are often used by banking related (but non-bank) holding entities and subsidiaries. These words are used specifically to avoid the restricted word "bank."

I find it rather curious that the New Zealand Companies Office did not simply add one letter and pick out the word "banco," which does in fact mean "bank" in Spanish, the second largest language in the world. Anyway, "banc" meaning "bank" or not in some unknown language, the Companies Office ordered every company with an already approved and registered company name containing any of the newly restricted words to change its name immediately, otherwise a forced name change would be performed simply using the company registration number as a new company name. Suffice to say, no company resolution, approval, or authorization of any kind by the board of directors or shareholders would be required. The Companies Office would simply edit the entries in the Company Register and change the names, and so they did. Those companies that had not responded to the threat, and thus not voluntarily effected a name change in time, found that their company names had been erased from one day to the next. Their company names had been replaced with their company registration numbers followed by "Limited." I have never seen nor heard of such a procedure anywhere else in the world, not even in cases in which companies in fact had the word "bank" in their names and were registered prior to such a word becoming restricted.

This is quite controversial if you think about it. A company is a legal person of its own in all aspects of the law, and it is identified mainly by its name, just like the rest of us. To all of a sudden change its name by force would obviously have serious consequences, especially for a company already doing business all over the world, holding bank accounts, being a party in executed contracts and agreements, owning properties and trademarks, and so on.

Many countries also have name restrictions for physical individuals, meaning that parents are not able to give just any name to their children. The main reason for these restrictions is that certain names are considered offensive and may cause suffering to the bearer. Naturally the restrictions are not the same in every country. These restrictions also change from time to time. Imagine if the authorities were all of a sudden to tell you to change your name immediately, or they would do it for you, owing to new name restrictions that apply retroactively. Worse still, imagine if you didn't choose a new name for yourself in time, and the authorities simply issued you with a number as your name. The comparison might seem like a bit of a stretch, but it would essentially entail many of the same implications and from a legal point of view, it is not a big leap.

Let us move on to the actual procedure of incorporating a New Zealand company online.

Start by going to companies.govt.nz:

1. Click on "Register".

2. Click on "Create your RealMe (formerly known as igovt) login now."

3. Provide your e-mail address and choose a username and password. The New Zealand phone number is not mandatory.

4. Choose three security questions and provide answers. This information is requested if you ever forget your password.

5. Accept the terms and conditions by ticking the box at the bottom of the screen.

6. Enter the letters in the security image and click "Create my RealMe login."

You now have a RealMe account that can be used for access to various government websites. Let us continue by creating a Companies Office user account:

1. Click on "Return to Companies Office".

2. Choose account type, individual or organization. An individual account is the most suitable for most users and can also be used to manage multiple companies.

3. Enter a name and address. If you are using a non-New Zealand address, click on "Manual or Overseas," enter the address, and then click on "Use this address." Click on "Continue".

4. Enter a phone number and a mailing address (if different from the physical address provided in the previous step), and tick the box for accepting the terms and conditions. Click on "Register".

5. You have the option to setup a direct debit arrangement for payment of registry fees. This only works when using a New Zealand bank

account. If you do not have a New Zealand bank account, tick the box for "No" and click "Continue". You will be able to pay fees using a credit or debit card issued in any country.

6. Done! You now have a Companies Office user account linked to your RealMe account. You will now be redirected to the incorporation interface. If the signup process is interrupted prior to completion for any reason, just log in with your RealMe credentials at companies.govt.nz. The process will then be resumed and you will be able to provide any missing information.

So let's incorporate, shall we? If you have been logged out, just log back in at companies.govt.nz to get to the main user dashboard. The first thing you need to do is to reserve a company name for your new entity.

1. Click on "Reserve a Company Name" in the left-hand side menu.

2. Enter the proposed company name ending with the word "Limited" (do not use the abbreviation Ltd at this point) and confirm.

3. Confirm acceptance of the fee (NZ$ 10.22) and click on Payment.

4. Enter debit or credit card information and click "Submit". You will receive an invoice by e-mail.

Company name approval will typically be obtained within one hour or less during New Zealand business hours. You will be notified by email once the name has been approved. After receiving approval, log back in at companies.govt.nz:

5. Click on "Start a Company"

6. Click on "Incorporate a NZ Company"

7. Choose your already approved name in the popup window and click on "Continue".

8. Enter the number of directors, shareholders and shares. You need a minimum of one director and one shareholder (this can be the same person). Directors must be physical individuals whereas shareholders can be either individuals or legal entities. Both directors and shareholders can be of any nationality and resident anywhere in the world. You can have any number of shares, but a common number would be one hundred or one thousand.

I suggest that you un-tick the box for tax registration. You can register for tax at any time. Click on "Next Step, Company Addresses."

9. Leave the option regarding management by a business professional un-ticked unless your company will be managed by a law firm, accountancy firm or the like.

Enter your New Zealand physical address to be used as the registered office. If the complete address does not show up in the automated search, click on "Enter Address Manually."

Address for service can be and usually is the same as the registered office, but if you prefer you can choose an alternative address for legal service and for communications.

Enter the company e-mail address and phone numbers (phone and fax are optional).

Choose filing month for the annual return and company renewal. This has nothing to do with tax return filing. It is simply the month in which you will be requested to reconfirm the company details each year starting the year after incorporation.

An address for share register is optional. You should only provide an address here if your share registers will not be kept at the registered office. Click on: Next Step, Directors.

10. Enter each director's first and last names completely and exactly as they appear in their passports or other government issued identification. Do not use initials. Be sure to use the director's complete physical residential address. Foreign directors will be asked for a certified copy of identification as well as a recent utility bill, so the address provided here must match the address on the utility bill. Further contact information is optional. Click on "Next Step, Shareholders."

11. Choose shareholders from the directors and/or provide new shareholders. Click on "Next Step, Share Allocations."

12. Enter share allocations. If you have only one shareholder, enter the total number of shares next to the name of the shareholder. Click on "Next Step, Constitution".

13. A constitution is optional and essentially sets out the rights, powers and duties of the company, the board and each director and shareholder. If a company is incorporated without

a constitution, its internal procedures are automatically governed by the Companies Act 1993. It can be helpful to have a constitution because banks and other third parties outside New Zealand often expect to see more company documents than just a certificate of incorporation and registry extract. Third parties might be used to seeing a "Memorandum and Articles of Association" or similar documentation used in other jurisdictions. The constitution will serve the same purpose as those documents. You can purchase and use a standard constitution from the Auckland District Law Society, www.adsl.org.nz or CCH, www.cchforms.co.nz, or you can proceed without a constitution.

14. Choose "I don't want to apply for a company IRD number (Tax ID) at this time." I suggest registering for tax later and to engage a New Zealand accountant for advice with regard to reporting requirements and tax liability. Click on "Next Step, GST Registration."

15. GST (sales tax) registration is not possible if you chose not to apply for an IRD number in the previous stage. A GST number can also be obtained later by you or your accountant. Click on "Next Step, Review."

16. Review your details and correct any errors if needed. Proceed to payment of the incorporation fee, NZ$150 in total. You will receive an invoice by email after completed payment.

17. Submit your application by clicking on "Incorporate."

18. You will receive consent forms by email. The forms need to be signed by the director(s) and shareholder(s) and returned by fax in accordance with the instructions on the form, or scanned and uploaded though the online user interface.

This used to be the end of the procedure. After uploading or faxing the consent forms in step 18, you would typically receive the certificate of incorporation and company registry extract by e-mail within minutes, and your company would be ready. As I mentioned earlier in this chapter, the Companies Office has adopted certain identification requirements after realizing that an anonymous company formation and registration procedure was not such a great idea after all. So instead of receiving an e-mail confirming your incorporation you are now more likely to receive a message asking for the following documents from each director and shareholder:

- The signed consent form in original

- Certified copy of a passport

- Certified copy of a recent utility bill (not older than three months)

If you do not have a passport, two pieces of other government issued identification will also be accepted, such as Social Security certificate and driver's license. Copies should be certified by lawyer, notary, or justice of the peace and include full contact details as well as the wording "True Certified Copy of the Original" or similar.

As previously mentioned, directors and shareholders can be of any nationality and can be resident anywhere in the world. You might nevertheless want to consider partnering up with or hiring someone in New Zealand who can act as a director. Your company will be met with less skepticism in New Zealand if you have a local director onboard. And besides, regulations will soon be introduced that will require a local director.

In today's world of social and business networking online, you should not find it too difficult to come across a prospective partner or employee in New Zeland.

You could also consider advertising in local newspapers or on local web sites such as hotfrog.co.nz and trademe.co.nz. You might also benefit from having a local shareholder, whether an individual or another legal entity. It is common to use an offshore holding company as sole shareholder but by doing so you trigger requirements to present audited financial statements to the Companies Office every year (see companies.govt.nz for further details about financial reporting requirements and other ongoing obligations).

You will also need a New Zealand registered office and to maintain certain records at this address. If you choose to have a company formation agent, accountancy firm or law firm incorporate your company for you they will typically also provide registered office services. If you incorporate yourself, you might want to sign up for a registered office address as a stand-alone service.

The following company can act as registered office and also provide regular mail-forwarding services:

Private Box Ltd.
24B Moorefield Rd.
Johnsonville
Wellington 6037

Phone: +64 4 831 1333
Fax: +64 4 831 1334
www.privatebox.co.nz

The following records need to be kept available for inspection at the registered office at all times:

- Constitution of the company (if one has been adopted)

- Minutes of all meetings and resolutions of shareholders and directors

- Share register and the directors' register

- All written communications to shareholders including annual reports

- Copies of all financial statements

- Accounting records for the current accounting period.

- All records must be held and updated regularly for the past seven years.

So what about taxation?

New Zealand introduced the "Look Through Company" (LTC) tax regime for limited companies in 2011, allowing for tax-free offshore operations.

A LTC must comply with the following:

1. Have five or fewer shareholders

2. Be a New Zealand resident for tax purposes

3. Issue only shares that have the same voting and participation rights

4. Have only natural persons or trustees as shareholders

The LTC is fiscally transparent and thus identical in its tax treatment to a partnership (and the U.S. LLC). Section BD 1(5)(c) of the Income Tax Act 2007 further provides an exemption from tax in New Zealand on income derived by a non-resident provided that income does not have its source in New Zealand. This means that a foreign shareholder of a LTC that only receives offshore income will not be subject to any tax in New Zealand.

Did I mention that there is no general capital gains tax in New Zealand nor any inheritance or estate taxes?

Most of the members of the anti-offshore crowd seem to be ignorant of the fact that New Zealand is quite a prominent offshore tax haven offering excellent zero tax structures. As a party to thirty-seven international double taxation agreements, New Zealand is generally perceived as a high-tax country and is thus usually not a target in the international campaign against tax havens.

One of the most popular offshore structures in New Zealand is the offshore trust, or foreign trust, which allows for a high level of privacy and absolute tax freedom. A foreign trust is one with a non-resident settlor and non-resident beneficiaries but with at least one local trustee, which can be an individual or a legal entity, for example a limited company or partnership. The New Zealand foreign trust is one of the most attractive asset protection and tax avoidance vehicles available today, especially considering the increasingly hostile attitude toward more traditional tax havens worldwide.

The tax-free trust regime has not eluded criticism entirely however. In a TV interview on New Zealand's TV3 edition of 60 Minutes that aired on September 7,

2012, revenue minister Peter Dunne was asked critical questions around the foreign trust concept. The local Green Party found the interview upsetting and immediately prepared a press release in which they criticized the trust regime as well as Dunne's defense of the same:

Revenue Minister Peter Dunne tonight endorsed tax avoidance as a legitimate practice when challenged about the use of secret New Zealand foreign trusts as a tax haven. TV3's 60 minutes highlighted problems with the trusts and Mr. Dunne responded that the behaviour was "legitimate tax avoidance." Mr. Dunne's repeated reference to legitimate tax avoidance was astounding. The tax system is being undermined by the minister in charge of it," Green Party co-leader Russel Norman said.

It seems as if Green Party co-leader Russel Norman has overlooked the fact that tax avoidance in most forms is indeed legitimate and legal, as opposed to tax evasion.

The media release continued:

New Zealand's foreign trust law allows non-residents to set up trusts here in New Zealand holding assets not liable for taxation. There are approximately 8000 foreign trusts registered with the Inland Revenue Department (IRD) holding assets estimated to be worth tens of billions of dollars. Little infor-

mation is required to register a foreign trust which means ownership is effectively anonymous and assets are invisible.

"New Zealand's foreign trusts hide billions of dollars of assets and should be broken open to help stop the global tax evasion industry," said Dr. Norman.

Foreign trusts established in New Zealand are not required to file income tax returns with the New Zealand Inland Revenue Department (IRD) if they do not have New Zealand source income and if no distribution has been made to a New Zealand resident beneficiary.

Notwithstanding the fact that no tax may be assessable in New Zealand, foreign trusts with resident trustees are still required to file disclosures to the IRD enabling the tax authority to keep track of their existence. Sufficient records are required to be kept in New Zealand to allow for assessable income, if any, to be determined. This requirement was implemented following a warning by the Australian Tax Office and specifically requires Australian resident settlors to be identified. The disclosed information can be made available under the exchange of information provisions of double tax agreements that New Zealand has with other countries. New Zealand does not maintain a central trust register, and considering the limited scope of the IRD disclosure requirements, one must conclude that New Zealand offers a high level of privacy and secrecy compared with many other jurisdictions.

In the case of trust structuring I strongly recommend the use of local professionals to enable the creation of a trust according to your specific conditions and requirements. Whereas companies can usually be formed using standard documentation allowing for the company to engage in any lawful activity, trusts typically require more specific structuring to be useful and to ensure compliance with the applicable regime.

I include contact information for some of the providers offering trust services in New Zealand here. As always, you can find many more online:

Turner Hopkins
Barristers & Solicitors
400 Lake Road
PO Box 33-237
Takapuna,
Auckland 0622
New Zealand
Phone: +649 486 2169
Fax: +649 486 2160
law@turnerhopkins.co.nz
www.turnerhopkins.co.nz

Queen City Law
Barristers & Solicitors
Level 8, 203 Queen Street
Auckland 1010
Phone: +649 970 8810
Fax: +649 970 8820
law@queencitylaw.co.nz
www.queencitylaw.co.nz

RLA Trustees Ltd
9-11 Galatos Street
Newton
Auckland 1010
Phone: +649 373 4383
Fax: +649 373 2199
principal@rlaltd.co.nz
www.rlatrustees.co.nz

New Zealand Trust & Investment Corporation
Level 2
8 Manukau Road
Newmarket
Auckland
Phone: +649 522 5214
Fax: +649 522 5215
info@newzealandtrustcorp.com
www.newzealandtrustcorp.com

The limited partnership (LP) introduced in 2008 provides for another potentially tax-free New Zealand structure. The LP is tax transparent, meaning that income passes through it without any tax assessment, just as in the case of the U.S. LLC and the U.K. LLP. The partners can be offshore entities or non-resident individuals who may not be subject to taxation on their foreign source income in their country of tax residence.

The Companies Office has been promulgating for several years that it will soon be possible to register a limited partnership (LP) online. They have yet to deliver on that promise as I write this book. Currently the only way to get an LP registered is by sending in physical paper forms. Nor are you able to find an existing LP in the regular company name search online. You must go to companies.govt.nz, click on "Online Services" and "Search Other Registries" in the menu. You will then be taken to a separate search interface, where you can tick the box for LPs and enter the relevant keywords. People trying to verify an LP online, such as a bank employee considering a new bank account application, commonly miss the somewhat obscure search function and thus conclude that the company in question cannot be found in the New Zealand Company Register. This is one of the minor disadvantages associated with an LP. Another is the meager company documentation provided by the registrar. While properly designed Certificates of Incorporation and Company Register Extracts can be downloaded at any time for regular limited companies, an LP is provided with a miserable looking Certificate of Registration by snail mail on registration. The certificate often looks like it has been sent through a chain of five or more fax machines before reaching your mailbox. This often prompts banks and others who might need to review your corporate documentation to question where the original Certificate of Registration is. Ordering a certified copy of the Certificate of Registration from the Companies Office can solve this issue. The certificate will still look as though it has been faxed around a few times but an original certification will be attached to it. Another factor to consider is that although the LP has gained popularity during the past few years, the regular limited company legal form is the most widely recognized.

So what are the advantages of an LP? There are actually several benefits, and they will likely compensate quite well for the disadvantages. The LP is a "pass-through" vehicle, meaning that the LP itself is not assessed for tax. The partners are responsible for any applicable taxation on their share of any profit. Non-resident partners can qualify to reap the benefits of New Zealand's various double taxation agreements. Offshore partners may not even be taxed on their foreign source income, depending on the rules in the home jurisdiction.

As previously mentioned, the regular limited companies can also be treated as pass-troughs under the recently introduced LTC regime, but only if they have physical individuals (a maximum of five) or trustees as shareholders. The LP has no such restrictions so partners can be either legal entities or physical individuals from any country.

Privacy can be another benefit of an LP. Information regarding general partners, who are responsible for all debts and liabilities of the LP, is publicly available in the LP Register. Information regarding limited partners, who are only responsible for their capital investment in the LP, is treated as confidential and is not publicly available.

You can find further information about the LP regime at this web address:

www.business.govt.nz/companies/learn-about/
other-entities/limited-partnerships

The registration form is very straightforward and simply needs to be filled out with the proposed name of the LP, its registered address in New Zealand and the names and addresses of the general and limited Partners (minimum of one each).

The registration form can be downloaded here:

www.business.govt.nz/companies/pdf-library/forms/limited-partnership-forms/form-lp1-pdf

Each general partner also needs to sign a consent form which can be downloaded here:

www.business.govt.nz/companies/pdf-library/forms/limited-partnership-forms/form-lp5-pdf

The proposed partners must certify that they have entered into a partnership agreement compliant with section 10 of the Limited Partnerships Act 2008.

A local lawyer can draft a partnership agreement or a compliant template can be purchased here:

www.zealandfinancial.co.nz/nz-limited-partnership

Note that although the partnership agreement is mandatory it does not have to be submitted to the registration authority.

Just as in the case of a limited company, the LP requires a New Zealand registered office at which basic records are kept with regard to partnership interests and accounting.

The government registration fee for a New Zealand LP is NZ$270 which can be paid by check or credit card.

A fine is a tax for doing something wrong.
A tax is a fine for doing something right.

author unknown

5

Traditional Offshores

The focus of this book is obviously the less traditional tax havens, the countries usually seen at the forefront of the international campaign against offshore tax avoidance and evasion. Nonetheless, I also find it relevant to mention the more traditional tax havens and the benefits they offer. You might consider structuring a U.S. LLC with a U.K. LLP as a sole member, or a U.K. LLP with two U.S. LLCs as partners, just to mention two possible scenarios of many. However, the traditional tax havens offer entities with less or no financial reporting requirements at all, in addition to total tax freedom on worldwide income. Such entities are attractive candidates for serving as LLC members and LLP or LP partners. By structuring for example a U.K. or U.S. Company with offshore tax haven partners, you get the best of both worlds: "onshore" presence and respectability combined with "offshore" privacy and tax freedom.

British overseas territories such as the British Virgin Islands, Bermuda, the Cayman Islands, and the Channel Islands are the among the ones figuring the most in the media at the time I write this book. This is logical since the UK has chosen to lead the campaign against offshore tax avoidance and can therefore be expected to do something about its own tax havens before attacking others. Unfortunately, as is so often the case, media reports have very little to do with reality.

I recently read an article stating that the tax haven days are over for the Cayman Islands. So how did the reporter come to this conclusion? The Cayman Islands can be considered one of the most important financial centers in the world, with more than 220 international banks holding in excess of US$1.5 trillion in assets. Out of the top fifty banks in the world, forty have a presence here. There are 140 licensed trust companies managing thousands of trusts. It is one of the most important jurisdictions for fund management, with more than thirty-five hundred regulated mutual funds and many more unregulated hedge funds. There are ninety-three thousand companies registered in the Cayman Islands, with nine thousand new registrations taking place every year.

So if the tax haven days in the Cayman Islands are over, what on earth happened? Can Cayman Island corporations no longer enjoy zero taxation on worldwide income? Yes, they can, and nothing has changed in this regard. Did they change the fund regulations and thereby provoke a mass migration of mutual funds and hedge funds? No, they did not. New fund registrations keep pouring in at the Monetary Authority.

What the reporter in question wanted to communicate was that the Cayman Islands signed a new Tax Information Exchange Agreement (TIEA), facilitating the exchange of information about U.S. bank account holders with the IRS. Although this is not in any way the first such agreement signed by the Caymans, one could agree that it is not good news for Americans hiding unreported funds in Cayman bank accounts. But does even the most ignorant reporter actually believe that the entire Cayman Islands financial sector revolves around Joe Tax Cheat from Palm Peach hiding some unreported cash from the IRS and his ex-wives in his offshore savings account? Perhaps the same reporter would think that the Forbes 500 corporations somehow "hide" their subsidiaries in the Caymans rather than openly report their existence to the Securities and Exchange Commission and everyone else who wants to know? Perhaps most readers of mainstream media have such a limited knowledge of the subject at hand that such reports will elude skepticism entirely. "Cayman Islands No Longer a Tax Haven." It sure sounds newsworthy, doesn't it?

Although I would not go as far as predicting that the false propaganda being spread around by media will turn into a self-fulfilling prophecy, there is of course a risk that it will affect the popularity of certain jurisdictions. I think the Caymans will remain a major tax haven for the foreseeable future. Nonetheless, I would undeniably prefer a less bullied jurisdiction than a U.K. overseas territory when currently choosing where to incorporate. Some traditional tax havens are simply less obvious targets in the "war on offshore" and offer the very same benefits.

Republic of Seychelles

Not one but 115 paradise islands in the Indian Ocean form the Republic of Seychelles, an independent democracy since 1976 with a history of both French and British rule.

The Seychelles offer traditional international business companies (IBCs) with zero tax on worldwide income and no reporting requirements. Companies are required to keep accounting records, but these can be kept anywhere in the world.

General Company Features

Type of company:	IBC
Type of law:	Hybrid
Typical time to establish a new company:	24 hrs
Corporate taxation:	Nil

Share capital

Standard currency:	USD
Permitted currencies:	Any
Minimum paid up capital:	US$ 1

Directors

Minimum number	1
Local director required:	No

Publicly accessible records:	No

Shareholders

Minimum number:	1
Publicly accessible records:	No

Company Secretary

Required:	No
Local or qualified:	No

Accounts

Requirements to prepare:	Yes
Audit requirements:	No
Requirements to file accounts:	No
Publicly accessible accounts:	No

Ongoing

Annual tax / renewal fee	US$ 100
Requirement to file annual return	No

Seychelles is very flexible when it comes to corporate name endings. The usual "Ltd," "Corp," "Inc." are all permitted, but more specific national suffixes, such as GmbH, AB, AG, BV, Pty Ltd, SA, and SARL, are also allowed.

Costs for formation should not exceed US$1000 and annual renewal fees starting the second year are often in the US$ 600-800 range, including resident agent and registered office fees. You can also find agents and law firms charging five times as much or more for a simple incorporation. Fancy law firms often charge exorbitant fees for simple company formations with the justification that each client requires specific structuring and consideration. In my experience, such firms simply resell standard company formations that they acquire cheaply from a local resident agent. The markup in price does not represent any added value or customized structuring of any kind. Firms that market company formations from a large number of jurisdictions all over the world are often among these overpriced operators running mere reseller operations. You can better choose a local, single-jurisdiction provider in each country where you form a company and pay reasonable fees without unnecessary markups. I have always received the best service from highly competitive IBC source providers charging less than a thousand dollars per company and often horrific service from the ones charging a lot more. This applies to most traditional offshore locales.

I include a few well-established source providers here:

Fidelity Corporate Services Ltd.
Suite 9 – Ansuya Estate
Revolution Avenue
Victoria - Mahe
Phone: +248 4610770
Fax: +248 4610771
www.seychellesoffshore.com

Abacus (Seychelles) Ltd.
Suite 3 - Global Village
Jivan's Complex
Mont Fleuri - Mahe
Phone: +248 461 0780
www.abacus-offshore.com

Intercontinental Trust (Seychelles) Ltd.
1st Floor Allied Plaza
Francis Rachel Street
Victoria – Mahe
Phone: +248 437 3689
Fax: +248 437 3299
www.intercontinentaltrust.sc

International Law & Corporate Services (Pty) Ltd.
2nd Floor Allied Building Annex
Francis Rachel Street
Victoria – Mahe
Phone: +248 432 3850
Fax: +248 422 5432
www.ilcssez.com

Hong Kong SAR

This former British territory is one of the most important trading hubs and financial centers in the world. Hong Kong was returned to China in 1997 after 156 years of British rule and became a Special Administration Region (SAR) within the People's Republic of China. Hong Kong has executive, legislative, and independent judicial power under the "one country, two systems" philosophy. The World Economic Forum has named Hong Kong the world's top financial center, and it currently holds the third position on the Global Financial Centres Index. One thing is certain: this jurisdiction no longer takes orders from London. To bully small tropical island countries is one thing, but who wants to bully China, a world superpower with population 1,361,770,000?

Hong Kong offers private limited companies with zero taxation on worldwide (non-Hong Kong source) income. Financial reporting requirements and, consequently, maintenance costs exceed what you would see in most traditional tax havens.

General Company Features

Type of company:	Private Limited
Type of law:	Common
Typical time to establish a new company:	2 days
Corporate taxation:	Nil

Share capital

Standard currency:	HKD
Permitted currencies:	Any
Minimum paid up capital:	HK$ 1

Directors

Minimum number	1
Local director required:	No
Publicly accessible records:	Yes

Shareholders

Minimum number:	1
Publicly accessible records:	Yes

Company Secretary

Required:	Yes
Local or qualified:	Local

Accounts

Requirements to prepare:	Yes
Audit requirements:	Yes
Requirements to file accounts:	Yes
Publicly accessible accounts:	No

Ongoing

Annual tax / renewal fee	HK$ 250
Requirement to file annual return	Yes

Considering the ongoing reporting requirements in Hong Kong you might consider engaging a full-service firm that also offers accounting services and tax advice. Here are some suitable firms offering a wide range of services, including accounting and local bank introductions:

CMS Corporate Management Services
1301 Bank of America Tower
12 Harcourt Road
Central – Hong Kong
Tel: +852 2115 9878
Fax: +852 2115 9818
www.cmshk.com

Bridges Executive Centre Ltd.
20th Floor
Central Tower
28 Queen's Road
Central - Hong Kong
Phone: +852 3665 7222
Fax: +852 3665 7288
www.bridges.hk

Edwin Cheung & Siu HK Accountants
Room A, 7/F
China Overseas Building
139 Hennessy Road
Wanchai - Hong Kong
Phone: +852 2851 1476
Fax: +852 2851 1480
www.cheungandsiu.com

Ras Al Khaimah (RAK), United Arab Emirates

The United Arab Emirates (UAE) consists of Abu Dhabi, Ajman, Dubai, Fujairah, Ras Al Khaima, Sharjah and Umm Al Quwain. There are thriving offshore regimes in the UAE, with Jebel Ali in Dubai, the largest free zone in the world, and RAK being the two most established. RAK is more competitive with regard to fees and offers more straight-forward procedures for corporate structuring.

RAK Offshore Companies offer all the benefits you can expect in a traditional offshore center. Corporate tax is zero, and you are not required to file accounts with any authority. Company details are not on public record, and 100 percent foreign ownership is allowed. RAK also offers investor visas for people looking to reside in the UAE. There is no personal income tax, and the UAE is one of the safest and wealthiest countries on the planet.

General Company Features

Type of company:	Limited
Type of law:	Federal
Typical time to establish a new company:	48 hrs
Corporate taxation:	Nil

Share capital

Standard currency:	AED
Permitted currencies:	AED, EUR, USD
Minimum authorized capital:	AED 10,000

Directors

Minimum number	1
Local director required:	No
Publicly accessible records:	No

Shareholders

Minimum number:	1
Publicly accessible records:	No

Company Secretary

Required:	Yes
Local or qualified:	No

Accounts

Requirements to prepare:	Yes
Audit requirements:	No
Requirements to file accounts:	No
Publicly accessible accounts:	No

Ongoing

Annual tax / renewal fee	US$ 100
Requirement to file annual return	No

Following are contact details of RAK offshore company formation agents:

EMN Chartered
Rakeen Bld.
Al Jazeera Al Hamra
Ras Al Khaimah, UAE
Phone: +971 4 3132819
Fax: +971 8 4683014
www.emndubai.com

Privacy Management Group FZ LLC
Amenity Center - Building No. 1
Upper Floor, Office No. 7/G
Al-Jazeera Al Hamra
Ras Al Khaimah, UAE
Phone: +971 4 453 2747
www.pmg-emirates.com

RAK Offshore
3rd Floor
The Meydan Office Tower
Executive Office
Dubai, UAE
Phone: +971 4 381 3738
Fax: +971 4 381 3739
www.rakoffshore.com

The UAE certainly makes an interesting option considering the political campaign against traditional tax havens. RAK is as offshore as tax havens come, but I doubt you have ever seen any anti-offshore activist attacking this jurisdiction. Look at how the United States blackmailed and pressured Swiss banks to give up banking secrecy. Virtually all Swiss bankers are threatened with U.S. prosecution simply because some of them have tax-evading Americans among their clients. A Swiss banker can be arrested when entering the United States (and several have been) simply because his clients did not comply with U.S. tax obligations. It is not in any way only the Swiss bankers who have actively conspired with U.S. clients to evade taxes that end up in serious legal trouble. The United States can and will impose withholding taxes on Swiss assets in the United States or worse, freeze the assets if the Swiss do not succumb and take responsibility for the tax crimes committed by their U.S. clients. Naturally, the result of this campaign is that most Swiss banks no longer accept American clients.

Can you imagine the United States applying the same type of blackmail tactics toward the UAE (major oil producer) or China (superpower)? Do you think the United States will ever start arresting UAE and Chinese citizens simply because they might have U.S.

clients? Such a scenario comes with totally different political and diplomatic implications. Of course, no politician would ever admit to this being the case. Without analyzing this inconsistency in detail, I think one can safely assume that offshore centers such as RAK will never be bossed around like Switzerland or the Caribbean rock-in-the-ocean jurisdictions.

One thing is certain: the offshore industry continues to flourish, and the more changes the rainy and cold impose on the sunny and warm, the more money offshore service providers will make while assisting their clients to adjust. One jurisdiction's loss is the other jurisdiction's gain. The need for constant adaptation to new rules and realities is indisputably what feeds the industry.

Feedback

Questions?

Comments?

Please Share!

readers@michaelmagnusson.com

Follow Michael Magnusson on Twitter for
Offshore Banking and Tax Haven News:

@magnussonwrites

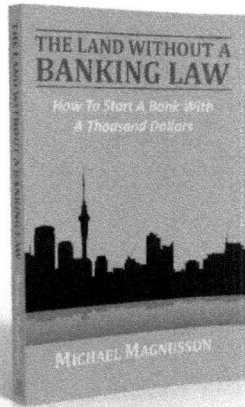

The Land without a Banking Law

How to Start a Bank with a Thousand Dollars

New Zealand is generally perceived as a high-tax country and has consequently not been a target in the international campaign against offshore tax havens. The fact is that New Zealand offers secretive zero tax structures for offshore activities, and perhaps even more remarkable, a legal framework that allows for virtually anyone to start a Bank without being subject to any capital or qualification requirements. New

Zealand Offshore Finance Companies are Banks, both in a legal and practical sense, but not Registered Banks under supervision of the Reserve Bank of New Zealand. While there are laws in New Zealand regulating financial activities, there are no regulatory entry barriers as such for the business of banking when services are offered to non-residents only. This book will teach you how to form and register a New Zealand Company online and how to obtain registration as a bona fide Financial Service Provider (FSP) with legal capacity to offer banking services to any number of clients, resident anywhere in the world. The regulatory framework and upcoming changes to the relevant legislation are explained.

Publisher:

Opus Operis LLP

Author:

Michael Magnusson

Paperback - 236 pages

ISBN-10: 0957543816
ISBN-13: 978-0957543812

Available through all major booksellers worldwide

Banking Law Bestseller on Amazon

APPENDIX

LLC Operating Agreement Sample

LIMITED LIABILITY COMPANY OPERATING AGREEMENT

SUNNY vs. SHADY LLC

A Member-Managed Limited Liability Company

OPERATING AGREEMENT

THIS OPERATING AGREEMENT is made and entered into effective (Month Day, Year), by and among: (Member Full Name), (Member Full Name), and (Member Full Name) (collectively referred to in this agreement as the "Members").

SECTION 1
THE LIMITED LIABILITY COMPANY

1.1 Formation

Effective (Month Day, Year), the Members form a limited liability company under the name Sunny vs. Shady L.L.C. (the "Company") on the terms and conditions in this Operating Agreement (the "Agreement") and pursuant to the Limited Liability Company Act of the State of _____ (the "Act"). The Members agree to file with the appropriate agency within the State of _____ charged with processing and maintaining such records all documentation required for the formation of the Company. The rights and obligations of the parties are as provided in the Act except as otherwise expressly provided in this Agreement.

1.2 Name

The business of the Company will be conducted under the name Sunny vs. Shady L.L.C., or such other name upon which the Members may unanimously may agree.

1.3 Purpose

The purpose of the Company is to engage in any lawful act or activity for which a Limited Liability Company may be formed within the State of

_____.

1.4 Office

The Company will maintain its principal business office within the State of _____ at the following address:

_____

_____

1.5 Registered Agent

(Full Name) is the Company's initial registered agent in the State of _____, and the registered office is:

_____

_____

1.6 Term

The term of the Company commences on (Month Day, Year) and shall continue perpetually unless sooner terminated as provided in this Agreement.

1.7 Names and Addresses of Members

The Members' names and addresses are attached as Schedule 1 to this Agreement.

1.8 Admission of Additional Members

Except as otherwise expressly provided in this Agreement, no additional members may be admitted to the Company through issuance by the company of a new interest in the Company without the prior unanimous written consent of the Members.

SECTION 2
CAPITAL CONTRIBUTIONS

2.1 Initial Contributions
The Members initially shall contribute to the Company capital as described in Schedule 2 attached to this Agreement.

2.2 Additional Contributions
No Member shall be obligated to make any additional contribution to the Company's capital without the prior unanimous written consent of the Members.

2.3 No Interest on Capital Contributions
Members are not entitled to interest or other compensation for or on account of their capital contributions to the Company except to the extent, if any, expressly provided in this Agreement.

SECTION 3
ALLOCATION OF PROFITS AND
LOSSES; DISTRIBUTIONS

3.1 Profits/Losses
For financial accounting and tax purposes, the Company's net profits or net losses shall be determined on an annual basis and shall be allocated to the Members in proportion to each Member's relative capital inter-

est in the Company as set forth in Schedule 2 as amended from time to time in accordance with U.S. Department of the Treasury Regulation 1.704-1.

3.2 Distributions

The Members shall determine and distribute available funds annually or at more frequent intervals as they see fit. Available funds, as referred to herein, shall mean the net cash of the Company available after appropriate provision for expenses and liabilities, as determined by the Managers. Distributions in liquidation of the Company or in liquidation of a Member's interest shall be made in accordance with the positive capital account balances pursuant to U.S. Department of the Treasury Regulation 1.704.1(b)(2)(ii)(b)(2). To the extent a Member shall have a negative capital account balance, there shall be a qualified income offset, as set forth in U.S. Department of the Treasury Regulation 1.704.1(b)(2)(ii)(d).

3.3 No Right to Demand Return of Capital

No Member has any right to any return of capital or other distribution except as expressly provided in this Agreement. No Member has any drawing account in the Company.

SECTION 4
INDEMNIFICATION

The Company shall indemnify any person who was or is a party defendant or is threatened to be made a party defendant, pending or completed action, suit or proceeding, whether civil, criminal, administrative, or investigative (other than an action by or in the right of the Company) by reason of the fact that he is or was a Member of the Company, Manager, employee or agent of the Company, or is or was serving at the request of the Company, against expenses (including attorney's fees), judgments, fines, and amounts paid in settlement actually and reasonably incurred in connection with such action, suit or proceeding if the Members determine that he acted in good faith and in a manner he reasonably believed to be in or not opposed to the best interest of the Company, and with respect to any criminal action proceeding, has no reasonable cause to believe his/her conduct was unlawful. The termination of any action, suit, or proceeding by judgment, order, settlement, conviction, or upon a plea of "no lo Contendere" or its equivalent, shall not in itself create a presumption that the person did or did not act in good faith and in a manner which he reasonably believed to be in the best interest of the Company, and, with respect to any criminal action or proceeding, had reasonable cause to believe that his/her conduct was lawful.

SECTION 5
POWERS AND DUTIES OF MANAGERS

5.1 Management of Company

5.1.1

The Members, within the authority granted by the Act and the terms of this Agreement shall have the complete power and authority to manage and operate the Company and make all decisions affecting its business and affairs.

5.1.2

Except as otherwise provided in this Agreement, all decisions and documents relating to the management and operation of the Company shall be made and executed by a Majority in Interest of the Members.

5.1.3

Third parties dealing with the Company shall be entitled to rely conclusively upon the power and authority of a Majority in Interest of the Members to manage and operate the business and affairs of the Company.

5.2 Decisions by Members

Whenever in this Agreement reference is made to the decision, consent, approval, judgment, or action of the Members, unless otherwise expressly provided in this Agreement, such decision, consent, approval, judgment, or action shall mean a Majority of the Members.

5.3 Withdrawal by a Member

A Member has no power to withdraw from the Company, except as otherwise provided in Section 8

SECTION 6
SALARIES, REIMBURSEMENT
AND PAYMENT OF EXPENSES

6.1 Organization Expenses

All expenses incurred in connection with organization of the Company will be paid by the Company.

6.2 Salary

No salary will be paid to a Member for the performance of his or her duties under this Agreement unless the salary has been approved in writing by a Majority of the Members.

6.3 Legal and Accounting Services

The Company may obtain legal and accounting services to the extent reasonably necessary for the conduct of the Company's business.

SECTION 7
BOOKS OF ACCOUNT, ACCOUNTING RE-PORTS, TAX RETURNS, FISCAL YEAR, BANKING

7.1 Method of Accounting

The Company will use the method of accounting previously determined by the Members for financial reporting and tax purposes.

7.2 Fiscal Year; Taxable Year

The fiscal year and the taxable year of the Company is the calendar year.

7.3 Capital Accounts

The Company will maintain a Capital Account for each Member on a cumulative basis in accordance with federal income tax accounting principles.

7.4 Banking

All funds of the Company will be deposited in a separate bank account or in an account or accounts of a savings and loan association in the name of the Company as determined by a Majority of the Members. Company funds will be invested or deposited with an institution, the accounts or deposits of which are insured or guaranteed by an agency of the United States government.

SECTION 8
TRANSFER OF MEMBERSHIP INTEREST

8.1 Sale or Encumbrance Prohibited

Except as otherwise permitted in this Agreement, no Member may voluntarily or involuntarily transfer, sell, convey, encumber, pledge, assign, or otherwise dispose of (collectively, "Transfer") an interest in the Company without the prior written consent of a majority of the other non-transferring Members determined on a per capita basis.

8.2 Right of First Refusal

Notwithstanding Section 8.1, a Member may transfer all or any part of the Member's interest in the Company (the "Interest") as follows:

8.2.1

The Member desiring to transfer his or her Interest first must provide written notice (the "Notice") to the other Members, specifying the price and terms on which the Member is prepared to sell the Interest (the "Offer").

8.2.2

For a period of 30 days after receipt of the Notice, the Members may acquire all, but not less than all, of the Interest at the price and under the terms specified in the Offer. If the other Members desiring to acquire the Interest cannot agree among themselves on the allocation of the Interest among them, the allocation will be proportional to the Ownership Interests of those Members desiring to acquire the Interest.

8.2.3

Closing of the sale of the Interest will occur as stated in the Offer; provided, however, that the closing will not be less than 45 days after expiration of the 30-day notice period.

8.2.4

If the other Members fail or refuse to notify the transferring Member of their desire to acquire all of the Interest proposed to be transferred within the 30-day period following receipt of the Notice, then the Members will be deemed to have waived their right to acquire the Interest on the terms described in the Offer, and the transferring Member may sell and convey the Interest consistent with the Offer to any other person or entity; provided, however, that notwithstanding anything in Section 8.2 to the contrary, should the sale to a third person be at a price or on terms that are more favorable to the purchaser than stated in the Offer, then the transferring Member must reoffer the sale of the Interest to the remaining Members at that other price or other terms; provided, further, that if the sale to a third person is not closed within six months after the expiration of the 30-day period describe above, then the provisions of Section 8.2 will again apply to the Interest proposed to be sold or conveyed.

8.2.5

Notwithstanding the foregoing provisions of Section 8.2, should the sole remaining Member be entitled to and elect to acquire all the Interests of the other Members of the Company in accordance with the provisions of Section 8.2, the acquiring Member may assign the right to acquire the Interests to a spouse, lineal descendent, or an affiliated entity if the assignment is reasonably believed to be necessary to continue the existence of the Company as a limited liability company.

8.3 Substituted Parties

Any transfer in which the Transferee becomes a fully substituted Member is not permitted unless and until:

(1) The transferor and assignee execute and deliver to the Company the documents and instruments of conveyance necessary or appropriate in the opinion of counsel to the Company to effect the transfer and to confirm the agreement of the permitted assignee to be bound by the provisions of this Agreement; and

(2) The transferor furnishes to the Company an opinion of counsel, satisfactory to the Company, that the transfer will not cause the Company to terminate for federal income tax purposes or that any termination is not adverse to the Company or the other Members.

8.4 Death, Incompetency, or Bankruptcy of Member

On the death, adjudicated incompetence, or bankruptcy of a Member, unless the Company exercises its rights under Section 8.5, the successor in interest to the Member (whether an estate, bankruptcy trustee, or otherwise) will receive only the economic right to receive distributions whenever made by the Company and the Member's allocable share of taxable income, gain, loss, deduction, and credit (the "Economic Rights") unless and until a majority of the other Members determined on a per capita basis admit the transferee as a fully substituted Member in accordance with the provisions of Section 8.3.

8.4.1

Any transfer of Economic Rights pursuant to Section 8.4 will not include any right to participate in management of the Company, including any right to vote, consent to, and will not include any right to information on the Company or its operations or financial condition. Following any transfer of only the Economic Rights of a Member's Interest in the Company, the transferring Member's power and right to vote or consent to any matter submitted to the Members will be eliminated, and the Ownership Interests of the remaining Members, for purposes only of such votes, consents, and participation in management, will be proportionately increased until such time, if any, as the transferee of the Economic Rights becomes a fully substituted Member.

8.5 Death Buy Out

Notwithstanding the foregoing provision of Section 8, the Members covenant and agree that on the death of any Member, the Company, at its option, by providing written notice to the estate of the deceased Member within 180 days of the death of the Member, may purchase, acquire, and redeem the Interest of the deceased Member in the Company pursuant to the provision of Section 8.5.

8.5.1

The value of each Member's Interest in the Company will be determined on the date this Agreement is signed, and the value will be endorsed on Schedule 3 attached and made a part of this Agreement. The value of each Member's Interest will be re-determined unanimously by the Members annually, unless the Members unanimously decide to re-determine those values more frequently. The Members will use their best efforts to endorse those values on Schedule 3. The purchase price for a decedent Member's interest conclusively is the value last determined before the death of such Member; provided, however, that if the latest valuation is more than two years before the death of the deceased Member, the provisions of Section 8.5.2 will apply in determining the value of the Member's Interest in the Company.

8.5.2

If the Members have failed to value the deceased Member's Interest within the prior two-year period, the value of each Member's Interest in the Company on the date of death, in the first instance, will be determined by mutual agreement of the surviving Members and the personal representative of the estate of the deceased Member. If the parties cannot reach an agreement on the value within 30 days after the appointment of the personal representative of the deceased Member, then the surviving Members and the personal representative each must select a qualified appraiser within the next succeeding 30 days. The appraisers so selected must attempt to determine the value of the Company Interest owned by the decedent at the time of death based solely on their appraisal of the total value of the Company's assets and the amount the decedent would have received had the assets of the Company been sold at that time for an amount equal to their fair market value and the proceeds (after payment of all Company obligations) were distributed in the manner contemplated in Section 8. The appraisal may not consider and discount for the sale of a minority Interest in the Company. In the event the appraisers cannot agree on the value within 30 days after being selected, the two appraisers must, within 30 days, select a third appraiser. The value of the Interest of the decedent in the Company and the purchase price of it will be the average of the two appraisals nearest in amount to one another. That amount will be final and binding on all parties and their respective successors, assigns, and representatives. The costs and expenses of the third appraiser and any costs and expenses of the appraiser retained but not paid for by the estate of the deceased Member will be offset against the purchase price paid for the deceased Member's Interest in the Company.

8.5.3

Closing of the sale of the deceased Member's Interest in the Company will be held at the office of the Company on a date designated by the Company, not be later than 90 days after agreement with the personal representative of the deceased Member's estate on the fair market value of the deceased Member's Interest in the Company; provided, however, that if the purchase price are determined by appraisals as set forth in Section 8.5.2, the closing will be 30 days after the final appraisal and purchase price are determined.

If no personal representative has been appointed within 60 days after the deceased Member's death, the surviving Members have the right to apply for and have a personal representative appointed.

8.5.4

At closing, the Company will pay the purchase price for the deceased Member's Interest in the Company. If the purchase price is less than $1,000.00, the purchase price will be paid in cash; if the purchase price is $1,000.00 or more, the purchase price will be paid as follows:

(1) $1,000.00 in cash, bank cashier's check, or certified funds;

(2) The balance of the purchase price by the Company executing and delivering its promissory note for the balance, with interest at the prime interest rate stated by primary banking institution utilized by the Company, its successors and assigns, at the time of the deceased Member's death. Interest will be payable monthly, with the principal sum being due and payable in three equal annual installments. The promissory note will be unsecured and will contain provisions that the principal sum may be paid in whole or in part at any time, without penalty.

8.5.5

At the closing, the deceased Member's estate or personal representative must assign to the Company all of the deceased Member's Interest in the Company free and clear of all liens, claims, and encumbrances, and, at the request of the Company, the estate or personal representative must execute all other instruments as may reasonably be necessary to vest in the Company all of the deceased Member's right, title, and interest in the Company and its assets. If either the Company or the deceased Member's estate or personal representative fails or refuses to execute any instrument required by this Agreement, the other party is hereby granted the irrevocable power of attorney which, it is agreed, is coupled with an interest, to execute and deliver on behalf of the failing or refusing party all instruments required to be executed and delivered by the failing or refusing party.

8.5.6

On completion of the purchase of the deceased Member's Interest in the Company, the Ownership Interests of the remaining Members will increase proportionately to their then-existing Ownership Interests.

SECTION 9
DISSOLUTION AND WINDING
UP OF THE COMPANY

9.1 Dissolution

The Company will be dissolved on the happening of any of the following events:

9.1.1

Sale, transfer, or other disposition of all or substantially all of the property of the Company;

9.1.2

The agreement of all of the Members;

9.1.3

By operation of law; or

9.1.4

The death, incompetence, expulsion, or bankruptcy of a Member, or the occurrence of any event that terminates the continued membership of a Member in the Company, unless there are then remaining at least the minimum number of Members required by law and all of the remaining Members, within 120 days after the date of the event, elect to continue the business of the Company.

9.2 Winding Up

On the dissolution of the Company (if the Company is not continued), the Members must take full account of the Company's assets and liabilities, and the assets will be liquidated as promptly as is consistent with obtaining their fair value, and the proceeds, to the extent sufficient to pay the Company's obligations with respect to the liquidation, will be applied and distributed, after any gain or loss realized in connection with the liquidation has been allocated in accordance with Section 3 of this Agreement, and the Members' Capital Accounts have been adjusted to reflect the allocation and all other transactions through the date of the distribution, in the following order:

9.2.1

To payment and discharge of the expenses of liquidation and of all the Company's debts and liabilities to persons or organizations other than Members;

9.2.2

To the payment and discharge of any Company debts and liabilities owed to Members; and

9.2.3

To Members in the amount of their respective adjusted Capital Account balances on the date of distribution; provided, however, that any then - outstanding Default Advances (with interest and costs of collection) first must be repaid from distributions otherwise allocable to the Defaulting Member pursuant to Section 9.2.3.

SECTION 10
GENERAL PROVISIONS

10.1 Amendments

Amendments to this Agreement may be proposed by any Member. A proposed amendment will be adopted and become effective as an amendment only on the written approval of all of the Members.

10.2 Governing Law

This Agreement and the rights and obligations of the parties under it are governed by and interpreted in accordance with the laws of the State of _____ (without regard to principles of conflicts of law).

10.3 Entire Agreement; Modification

This Agreement constitutes the entire understanding and agreement between the Members with respect to the subject matter of this Agreement. No agreements, understandings, restrictions, representations, or warranties exist between or among the members other than those in this Agreement or referred to or provided for in this Agreement. No modification or amendment of any provision of this Agreement will be binding on any Member unless in writing and signed by all the Members.

10.4 Attorney Fees

In the event of any suit or action to enforce or interpret any provision of this Agreement (or that is based on this Agreement), the prevailing party is entitled to recover, in addition to other costs, reasonable attorney fees in connection with the suit, action, or arbitration, and in any appeals. The determination of who is the prevailing party and the amount of reasonable attorney fees to be paid to the prevailing party will be decided by the court or courts, including any appellate courts, in which the matter is tried, heard, or decided.

10.5 Further Effect

The parties agree to execute other documents reasonably necessary to further effect and evidence the terms of this Agreement, as long as the terms and provisions of the other documents are fully consistent with the terms of this Agreement.

10.6 Severability

If any term or provision of this Agreement is held to be void or unenforceable, that term or provision will be severed from this Agreement, the balance of the Agreement will survive, and the balance of this

Agreement will be reasonably construed to carry out the intent of the parties as evidenced by the terms of this Agreement.

10.7 Captions

The captions used in this Agreement are for the convenience of the parties only and will not be interpreted to enlarge, contract, or alter the terms and provisions of this Agreement.

10.8 Notices

All notices required to be given by this Agreement will be in writing and will be effective when actually delivered or, if mailed, when deposited as certified mail, postage prepaid, directed to the addresses first shown above for each Member or to such other address as a Member may specify by notice given in conformance with these provisions to the other Members.

IN WITNESS WHEREOF, the parties to this Agreement execute this Operating Agreement as of the date and year first above written.

MEMBERS:

_____

(Member Full Name)   Signature

_____

(Member Full Name)   Signature

_____

(Member Full Name)   Signature

Listing of Members - Schedule 1

LIMITED LIABILITY COMPANY
OPERATING AGREEMENT FOR

SUNNY vs. SHADY, L.L.C.

LISTING OF MEMBERS

As of the (Day) day of (Month, Year), the following is
a list of Members of the Company:

NAME   ADDRESS

_____

_____

_____

_____

Authorized by Member(s) to provide Member Listing
as of this (Day) day of (Month, Year).

_____

(Member Full Name)   Signature

_____

(Member Full Name)   Signature

_____

(Member Full Name)   Signature

APPENDIX

Listing of Capital Contributions - Schedule 2

LIMITED LIABILITY COMPANY
OPERATING AGREEMENT FOR

SUNNY vs. SHADY L.L.C.

CAPITAL CONTRIBUTIONS

Pursuant to ARTICLE 2, the Members' initial contribution to the Company capital is stated to be $100. The description and each individual portion of this initial contribution is as follows:

NAME   CONTRIBUTION   OWNERSHIP

SIGNED AND AGREED this (Day) day of (Month, Year).

_____

(Member Full Name)   Signature

_____

(Member Full Name)   Signature

_____

(Member Full Name)   Signature

Listing of Valuation of Members Interest
Schedule 3

LIMITED LIABILITY COMPANY
OPERATING AGREEMENT FOR

SUNNY vs. SHADY L.L.C.

VALUATION OF MEMBERS INTEREST

Pursuant to ARTICLE 8, the value of each Member's interest in the Company is endorsed as follows:

NAME   VALUATION ENDORSEMENT

(Member Full Name)	$100
(Member Full Name)	$100
(Member Full Name)	$100

_____

(Member Full Name)   Signature

_____

(Member Full Name)   Signature

_____

(Member Full Name)   Signature

Feedback

Questions?

Comments?

Please Share!

readers@michaelmagnusson.com

Follow Michael Magnusson on Twitter for
Offshore Banking and Tax Haven News:

@magnussonwrites